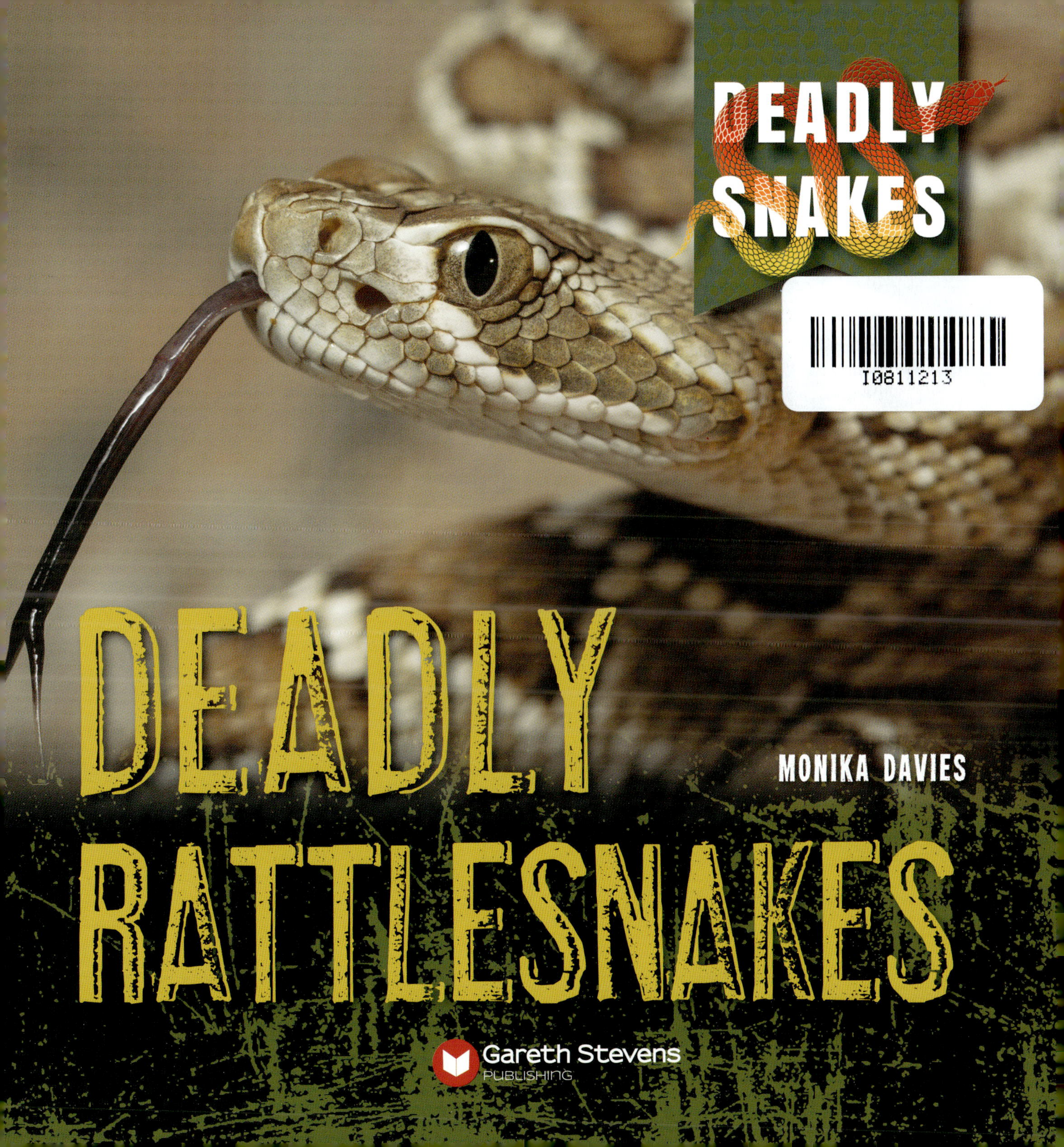

DEADLY SNAKES

DEADLY RATTLESNAKES

MONIKA DAVIES

Gareth Stevens PUBLISHING

Please visit our website, www.garethstevens.com. For a free color catalog of all our high-quality books, call toll free 1-800-542-2595 or fax 1-877-542-2596.

Library of Congress Cataloging-in-Publication Data
Names: Davies, Monika, author.
Title: Deadly rattlesnakes / Monika Davies.
Description: New York : Gareth Stevens Publishing, [2023] | Series: Deadly snakes | Includes index.
Identifiers: LCCN 2021050751 (print) | LCCN 2021050752 (ebook) | ISBN 9781538279847 (set) | ISBN 9781538279854 (library binding) | ISBN 9781538279830 (paperback) | ISBN 9781538279861 (ebook)
Subjects: LCSH: Rattlesnakes–Juvenile literature. | Poisonous snakes–Juvenile literature.
Classification: LCC QL666.O69 D385 2023 (print) | LCC QL666.O69 (ebook) | DDC 597.96/38–dc23/eng/20211201
LC record available at https://lccn.loc.gov/2021050751
LC ebook record available at https://lccn.loc.gov/2021050752

First Edition

Portions of this work were originally authored by Shaye Reynolds and published as *Rattlesnakes.* All new material in this edition authored by Monika Davies.

Published in 2023 by
Gareth Stevens Publishing
29 E. 21st Street
New York, NY 10010

Designer: Sheryl Kober
Editor: Monika Davies

Photo credits: Cover, p. 1 Alexander Wong/Shutterstock.com; cover (snake illustration) vinap/Shutterstock.com; cover, pp. 1–24 (background texture) Anna Timoshenko/Shutterstock.com; pp. 1–24 (snakeskin) Natalliya85/Shutterstock.com; pp. 1–24 (halftone texture) MPFphotography/Shutterstock.com; pp. 4, 16, 19 (snake illustration) vinap/Shutterstock.com; pp. 7, 8, 11, 15, 20 (fatal facts texture) Pakhnyushchy/Shutterstock.com; p. 5 Ali Iyoob Photography/Shutterstock.com; pp. 6, 21 Creeping Things/Shutterstock.com; p. 9 woodphotography LLC/Shutterstock.com; p. 10 Chief Design/Shutterstock.com; p. 12 Eric Isselee/Shutterstock.com; p. 13 Maria Dryfhout/Shutterstock.com; p.14 muuraa/Shutterstock.com; p. 17 Chase Clausen/Shutterstock.com; p. 18 Joe McDonald/Shutterstock.com.

Printed in the United States of America

CPSIA compliance information: Batch #CSGS23: For further information contact Gareth Stevens, New York, New York, at 1-800-542-2595.

CONTENTS

Words in the glossary appear in **bold** type the first time they are used in the text.

THE ALARMING RATTLESNAKE

On a grassland, a long snake lies hidden under a gray rock. This hunter is on the lookout for something to eat. A mouse darts in front of the snake—and with a quick snap of its head, the snake strikes, sinking its teeth into the small **mammal**. Gulp! The mouse is eaten whole!

Meet the rattlesnake, a clever—and deadly—predator that lives throughout North America. They are best known for the rattle on the tip of their tail.

Rattlesnakes are known for their rattle and their venomous bite. This means they can produce a liquid called venom that is harmful to other animals.

Most rattlesnakes are a gray or light brown color. But there are some rattlesnakes that are orange, pink, red, or green!

SPY THE RATTLESNAKE

Adult rattlesnakes come in a wide range of lengths. They can be as short as 1 foot (0.3 m) or as long as 8 feet (2.4 m)! The heaviest rattlesnake in the world is the eastern diamondback rattlesnake. This snake can weigh up to 10 pounds (4.5 kg).

Rattlesnakes have a triangle-shaped head. The different patterns on their skin help them blend in with their **habitat.** Western diamondback rattlesnakes and eastern diamondback rattlesnakes both have a diamond pattern on their skin.

FATAL FACTS

There are over 30 species, or kinds, of rattlesnake. You can tell them apart by their different sizes, colors, and patterns. However, they all have a rattle on the tip of their tail.

A RATTLER'S LIFESTYLE

Rattlesnakes usually don't spend much time with each other. They are solitary animals, which means they often live and hunt alone. However, many rattlesnakes live in dens together during the winter. Female rattlesnakes sometimes come together while they are **pregnant** and after giving birth.

Rattlesnake mothers usually give birth to their babies around the summertime. Unlike some snakes, rattlesnakes don't lay eggs. Their babies are born alive and wrapped in a clear covering. When they break out, they're ready to hunt.

FATAL FACTS

Baby rattlesnakes have a venomous bite too. They may be hunters, but they have to watch out! Birds and coyotes would love to eat them.

Newborn rattlesnakes have what's called a button at the tip of their tails. It grows into a rattle as they get older.

WHERE WESTERN RATTLESNAKES LIVE

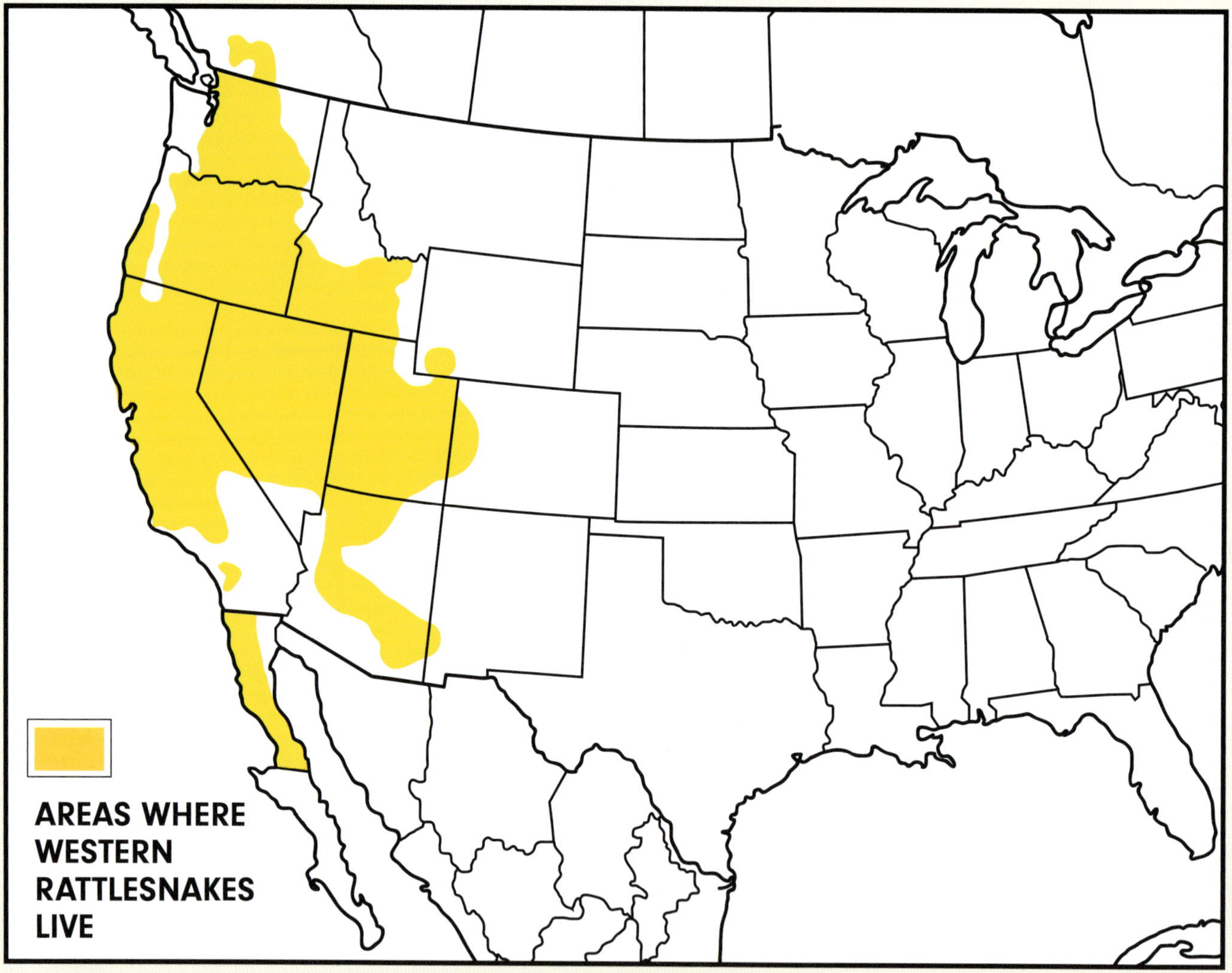

Out of all rattlesnake species, the western rattlesnake has one of the largest ranges in North America. This map shows all the regions where they live.

WHERE ARE THE RATTLESNAKES?

Rattlesnakes are found all over North America and South America. Western diamondback rattlesnakes live in many U.S. states, including Arizona, New Mexico, California, and Texas. Prairie rattlesnakes are found in midwestern states and in southern Canada in addition to northern Mexico. Eastern diamondback rattlesnakes make their home in the southeastern U.S. states of North Carolina, Florida, Mississippi, and Louisiana.

Rattlesnakes live in many different habitats. They live and hunt in grasslands, woodlands, swamps, and meadows. Some are found in rocky hills or on the coast.

FATAL FACTS

Many rattlesnakes are found in the desert. If you're walking in the American Southwest or central Mexico, watch out for the Mojave rattlesnake!

STRONG SENSES

Rattlesnakes are skilled hunters with many super senses. They can feel vibrations, or small, quick movements, on the ground.

Rattlesnakes pick up smells with their tongue. Then, their tongue passes the smells to a special body part called the Jacobson's **organ** on the roof of their mouth. This part recognizes the smell. Rattlesnakes have other special body parts called pit organs between their **nostrils** and eyes. These pits help rattlesnakes sense the heat of objects around them. This gives them the ability to "see" their **prey** at night!

Did you know rattlesnakes are also great swimmers? They've been spotted out at sea.

Rattle, rattle! A rattlesnake can shake its rattle up to 90 times per second.

HEAR THE RATTLE

Most animals stay far, far away from rattlesnakes. However, there are a few animals that dare to approach them. Luckily, the rattlesnake has a special **defense**—its rattle.

When a rattlesnake sees a possible predator, it shakes its rattle quickly. The rattle is made of keratin, which is what your fingernails are made of. The hollow segments, or parts, click together to make the rattling sound. This sound tells predators to stay away. But they may bite without rattling first if given no other choice!

FATAL FACTS

Each time a rattlesnake molts, or sheds its skin, a new segment forms on its rattle. The segments chip and break over time.

SPECIALIZED PREDATOR

Rattlesnakes are specialized predators that mainly eat small **rodents**. They love to hunt small mammals, such as mice, rats, and squirrels. However, rattlesnakes sometimes go after lizards, bugs, and even small birds that are on the ground.

Even as deadly predators, rattlesnakes have their own predators to worry about. Big birds, such as hawks and eagles, swoop down to catch small rattlesnakes. Kingsnakes are large snakes known to eat rattlesnakes. Coyotes and bobcats will also pick a fight with this rattling hunter.

Young rattlesnakes mainly eat lizards.

Like many snakes, rattlesnakes can eat just one meal every couple of weeks!

ON THE HUNT

Rattlesnakes usually hunt during evening and early morning hours. On hot days, the snake curls up in its hiding place. By late evening, it's time to hunt. The rattlesnake leaves its den and **slithers** along the ground.

When the rattlesnake finds its prey, it waits for the moment to strike. It sinks its fangs, or long, pointed teeth, into the animal. Venom that can be deadly flows through the hollow fangs. Then, it's time to eat!

CARING FOR THE RATTLESNAKE

Many people find the rattlesnake a terrifying hunter. However, these snakes are more shy than scary. Rattlesnakes only bite humans if they are feeling scared.

In contrast, humans are the greatest danger to rattlesnakes. As cities grow, many rattlesnakes have lost their homes. Rattlesnakes are often hit by cars as they warm themselves lying on roads. People also sometimes hunt rattlesnakes out of fear. But these predators are a key part of the **ecosystem**. Rattlesnakes aren't an **aggressive** snake species—and they need our help to stay safe.

FATAL FACTS

Most rattlesnake bites happen when a person tries to pick up a rattlesnake or touches one by mistake. People rarely die from rattlesnake bites, but it's important to get to the hospital right away.

Most rattlesnakes just want to be left alone. If a rattlesnake does bite, you can take a special drug called antivenin (also called antivenom).

GLOSSARY

aggressive: showing a readiness to attack

defense: a way of guarding against an enemy

ecosystem: all the living things in an area

habitat: the natural place where an animal or plant lives

mammal: a warm-blooded animal that has a backbone and hair, breathes air, and feeds milk to its young

nostril: an opening through which an animal breathes

organ: a part inside an animal's body

pregnant: carrying an unborn baby in the body

prey: an animal that is hunted by other animals for food

region: a large area of land that has features that make it different from nearby areas of land

rodent: a small, furry animal with large front teeth, such as a mouse or rat

slither: to slide easily over the ground

FOR MORE INFORMATION

Books

Coupé, Jessica. *Rattlesnakes.* New York, NY: AV2, 2021.

Sprott, Gary. *Western Diamondback Rattlesnake.* North Mankato, MN: Rourke Educational Media, 2019.

Websites

National Geographic Kids: Rattlesnakes

kids.nationalgeographic.com/animals/reptiles/facts/rattlesnake

Watch a quick video and discover more about rattlesnakes here.

San Diego Zoo Wildlife Explorers: Rattlesnakes

kids.sandiegozoowildlifealliance.org/animals/rattlesnake

Learn more fun facts about rattlesnakes on this website.

INDEX